The Knots of Pinkie Fingers

Kundu and Smriti

CONTENTS

PREFACE

This book began as a quiet conversation between two old friends. We've been sharing our poems since our school days, long before life became crowded with studies, careers, and the daily rush of living. After years of drifting through our separate worlds, we found each other again last year, and our discussion turned to the passion that had always connected us—poetry. From that conversation came a realisation: it was time to gather our best work and offer it to the world, a collection of the words that have shaped us, challenged us, and brought us back to ourselves.

We believe that love is the best state of being. It is the most meaningful thing to do, the most worthwhile path to walk. In every season of life—through its joys and sorrows—love remains a powerful force, grounding and transformative, capable of turning even the darkest moments into light. This collection, The Knot of Pinkie Fingers, is a poetic odyssey through the many shades of love and life, capturing everything from the first flutter of young love to the profound depths of mature and revolutionary love.

Within these pages, you'll find poems that celebrate the beauty of nature, wildlife, and art while also exploring the richness of culture, the necessity of collaboration, and the enduring importance of human values. In every line, we've tried to reflect the complexity of human connection—a journey from soft whispers to bold declarations, from personal longings to shared dreams of a world in harmony.

We are deeply grateful to everyone who has been part of our journey—our elders, our siblings, our friends, and all the people who have loved us, supported us, and inspired us. Their presence and influence are woven into every verse, a testament to the bonds that have shaped us and our work.

We hope that as you turn these pages, you will experience a rollercoaster of emotions, feeling the full spectrum of what it means to be human. Our poems are written In a language that is simple and unadorned, with no desire to force any opinion, but rather to invite you into a space where you can explore your own thoughts and feelings.

So, we ask you to begin this journey with an open heart. Come along with us without judgment, and let these poems wash over you, allowing yourself to simply be in the moment, to feel, to remember, and to dream.

May this collection bring you as much joy in reading as it has brought us in creating.

SORRY

Hello Lioness,

I hope you are basking in the pink of your happiness. There is so much I never said, and perhaps I should or shouldn't have, but here are a few things that I could say. When I first saw you, I was blown away and promised myself that I would do whatever it takes to make you smile. However, I messed up, maybe due to immaturity or stupidity, and for that, I am truly sorry. It was never my intention to disrupt your beautiful life, but for a moment or more, I did. Thankfully, it didn't affect you greatly, but I lost your trust in me. I feel ashamed for not doing enough for the person I should've cherished.

I want to express my gratitude for what I achieved through your love. Your love set me free, aiding my understanding of the universe and helping me battle my ego. It's still helping me become a better person day by day. Loving you changed my life, and it continues to do so. I had never felt this way before meeting you, and your love assisted me in navigating various life situations.

I'm blessed for the joy your love brought me, something I can never repay. I apologise for not sharing what I should have, leaving me crippled or cowardly.

While I always claimed to be there for you, I failed to make you feel that way. I never informed you that I could save your soul, just as you are capable of saving mine. I neglected to support you during your difficult times.

I'm sorry for not making you mine, for not pretending, not playing tricks, not showcasing only my good side, and not hiding things like most people do. I apologise for just loving you, as I know it was insufficient to significantly improve your life or convince you that someone is there for you no matter what.

I want to tell you to go for it, Garal. Believe it or not, you are amazing, and nothing can stand in your way. You will conquer everything. If you ever need anything or simply want to talk, I am here and will always be.

Thank you for everything, and sorry for loving you minimally.

Ram Ram

BEYOND INFINITY

Every morning, my love for you is twice what it was the previous night. Every evening, it is thrice what it was in the morning. Every night, my pain is ten times what it was the previous night. Now, I realise what is beyond infinity.

WE DON'T TALK ANYMORE

The larynx vibrates, and it produces sound,
They say stuff about, uh, about me, about us;
People talk,
But we don't talk anymore...
The time we spent together is unforgettable,
It was the best for me; maybe not for, uh,
We had issues; we had fights,
But are you happy now?
We don't fight anymore...

I'm fine... actually, good,
But we don't talk anymore,
Separating and wishing each other
happiness is the stupidest thing... If you
want her to be happy, then don't separate,
And if you can see her happy without you and you do not
evaporate...
Sorry, you never loved her as much as you claim.
Yeah, true love always wins,
But I don't believe it anymore...
We both want to,
But we don't talk anymore...
The last time I felt my body was when we hugged,
The last time I felt my hand was when you held it,

The last time I felt my steps were coming towards you. The last thing I heard was you calling my name. The last thing I noticed was you staring at me...

Everything else is just everything,

It's I don't give a FUCK anymore. We can get our souls back by doing so, but we don't talk anymore.

Yeah, days are usually good; Sometimes not. Now my nerves remain cool, sometimes hot.

But the time between dusk and dawn

is about you, you and you.

I dance, I sing, I laugh,

But I don't smile anymore.

People will ask about our story,

And all we have to say is,

"We don't talk anymore..."

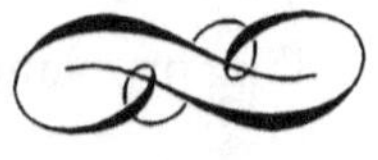

TRUE BANK

There are completely different seasons over there,
I will wait for you on the other side of the river.

YOU ARE ENOUGH

Stay there and fuck your life,
I am enough to fuck mine;
Or show some courage
And come forward,
Ask me to save your soul,
Baby, you are enough to save mine.

PILGRIMAGE

Her curves are the waves. Her navel is the vortex. She has the divine flow. She is my river.

She looks like an endearing deer. She dances like a peacock. She walks like a lioness. She is my forest.

Her skin is the fertile soil. Her lips are roses. Her scent is of jasmine. She is my garden.

Her eyes are a mirage. Her smile is an oasis. Her words are like cacti. She is my desert.

Her tresses have that darkness. Her face has that moonlight. Planets orbit around her fingers. She is my Milky Way.

Her body is my temple. Her heart is my God. Her love is my faith. She is my pilgrimage.

OH DIVINE

"Hey, listen, you divine being of heaven. I love you like hell."

BABE

Lakes, oceans, rivers, brooks
waterfalls, sand dunes, trees and rocks
I see everything within just two eyes
and you are asking me to explain it in just two lines;
Hundreds of languages, millions of vocab and this great
literature and heavy books
Burn 'em, babe,
They don't have a single word of your match.
Maybe you aren't the most beautiful girl on earth,
But, ever since I saw you, I don't give a fuck about the most
beautiful girl on earth.
This sunset blood sky and its reflection in the water; these
lotuses, lilies and little ducks,
Fuck 'em, babe,
There is no scenery without you,
Why should we agree with anyone?
Why do we have to believe anything? Why should we live as
told by someone in sometime according to something?
These fake sects, superstitions, brainless scholars, societies and
moral values
Deny 'em, babe;
One religion, true religion, is LOVE.
You are so lovely, too easy to love; many of
them must be in love with you, but trust
me, none of them is in love with you;

most of them could be handsome,
charming or crazy rich.
I am nothing like 'em, but I have a life for uh
These diamond rings, these necklaces
Platinum bands and white gold,
Trash 'em, babe,
I have my heart for you;
Don't tell me that these colourful petals are to welcome the
honeybees
Don't show me how flowers are kissed by
honeybees. Keep a vessel of sugar syrup near
their hives and see the love of your honeybees
These Romeos, Ranjhas, Mirzas, Mahiwals
Or whoever claims true love for you
Tell 'em, babe,
A boy gonna love you like nobody else
Why don't you notice the love in my eyes?
Why can't you see the changing colours of my face?
Why don't you listen to the scream of my heart?
Darling, you flow in the blood in my every vein,
These dancing feet, this floating heart.
On songs by Selena Gomez and Babbu Maan
Hold 'em, babe,
I am dancing in pain; I am dancing in the dark,
Your glow is so irresistible, it is so hard to look at you and not
to look at you.
You are the ultimate intoxication, darling
I lost my senses forever.
Girl, I have found divine light in the darkness under your tresses,
Your eyes are a maze, and your smile is magic
Your cheeks are wonder your lips are wow
Keep 'em, babe

But the best part is your ugly nose
Bricks on bricks, rooms and halls, stories and
stairs, Skyscrapers of NYC destroy 'em, darling.
I find my place between your arms. Cross your
fingers with mine, grab me like a baby grabs
her mother; my dream is to walk with you
barefoot on grass. Goose down feather,
baby cashmere, finest velvet, the great Indian
silk;
Remove 'em, babe
My pillow is your bosom,
You are the thing I am so sure about,
I look at you and see my future,
I am full of anger and bleat
But my protest ends at your cwtch,
Oh, girl, I die every single fucking time you le
Every time you came back was rebirth,
Flagon of your neck, curves you got
This silver body, this diamond face
Melt 'em, babe,
I am in love with the mud of your heart.

ANSWER ME

"Why do I always look at you like an infant looks at everything—carefully and with surprise?"

BEFORE THE DAY YOU WERE BORN

I've seen the sun sinking in the water,

I've seen that orange supermoon,

I've seen snowfall in the Himalayas,

I've seen herons flying in dark clouds,

I've seen turtles, fish, swans, and snakes swimming in the green water of the pond,

I've seen tiny droplets of dew on the leaves,

I've seen raindrops scattering and hitting the ground, and Devraaj Inder's Bow is that rainfall.

I've seen the pure water of the River Ganga in the mountains.

I've seen vortexes in the Yamuna.

I've seen the varnishing golden crop of wheat in the northern plains.

I've seen the sharp blades of jowar,

I've seen standing plants of pearl millet,

I've seen fresh, hot, melting jaggery,

I've seen the blossoming yellow mustard flowers,

I've seen cotton balls rupturing in the month of August,

Believe me, babe, these things were very beautiful before the day you were born.

AL PACINO

I saw him lighting a Gold Flake under a shed on a rainy day. Since then, I have forgotten everything about Al Pacino.

REASON FOR LOVE

"I love you for no reason." It's so stupid. You can't truly love anyone without a reason. If that's the case, you could fall in love with anyone and everyone.

"I love you for a reason." Maybe it's your beautiful face. Yes, I see hundreds of beautiful faces every day, but none have the same sparkle as yours.

It might be your alluring eyes, which shine brighter than the Kohinoor.

It could be your lips where the entire silence of the universe lounges.

Maybe it's your cheeks where cuteness enjoys its existence.

It can be your flicks that make my fingers feel crippled

It could be your walk with that my entire universe comes and walks away

Or your attitude that encompasses both Everest's peak and the depths of the Pacific.

It could be all of these reasons or none at all.

But you were created by Venus thyself and created to be loved.

Your absence leaves me restless; your presence makes me feel alive.

Your ignorance makes me feel lifeless, while your attention li s me to the divine.

Waiting for you is the most wonderful feeling.

Seeing you blush because of me makes me feel valued.

My heart races and my throat becomes dry when I'm near you.
I have to contemplate countless times before speaking to you.
But I can't tolerate a word against you.
I'd burn the whole world for you, but my fuse explodes in front of you.
I've spent my whole life wondering, yet I can't find the reason.
Perhaps only you can make me feel alive and dead at the same time.
And I, I bow only to you because you are you, and nothing is above you.

EXPERIMENT

After creating this universe, God tried every possible experiment to create the most beautiful thing, and at last, he succeeded in creating you."

THE POEM

Laying on the cot, on rooftop under the moon
Someone whispered in my ear, "Hey, poet! Get up soon,"
Was in your dreams don't want to open my eyes
I asked her, "Can't you wait till the sunrise?"
"Oye, don't you listen?" now, she asked loudly
"I am the poem 'THE POEM'," she said proudly
"'The Poem'? What is so special about you? Are you by Keats or
Frost?
By sage Vyas or Tulsidas ?"
"Stupid, I am that poem which would describe her beauty."
"Leave it, babe. That's not your cup of tea."
"I'll do anything for it,"
She persisted, "I'll do it,"
"Look, I respect your pertinacity,
But it's not possible for your perversity."
Did I bless her with the right words?
I am a poet and make a poem unnerved
Else, what I could do
Is it possible for a poem ??
Just a poem to describe you
She can't
Maybe I am disgracing her, but
She can't
How could she

Because

The poem doesn't know the art of getting engrossed in the scent of your hair and then escaping from it. How could she get unlocked from the lock of your tresses,

Would you allow her to kiss the gleam of your front

Would the sword of your sharp eyebrows show mercy to her

Can she look through the lance of your alluring eyes, or can she make the eyelashes cumbersome, which is sentry to them? Does she have the courage to punch your ugly nose that releases the warm breath or to eat the apple of your cheeks? Would you let her osculate your pink lips or exchange the taste buds?

Can she sing a song to please your eardrums? Does she know that much mathematics that she could count your teeth and the smile they spread by smiling? She has to pass over through the flagon of your neck and canoodle your back,

She has to cut through the blade of your shoulder,

Have to reveal the secret of the bone of your collar,

Does she have the patience to sleep on your small white bosom

And hear the peaceful music of your heart?

She has to run through the line of tiny treasure trails that run between your navel and vulva.

She can't give a signature on your labia

Oh right!! Would you stop her from jumping in the honeypot

Hold her in your hand,

Could she see my fate rising in the lines of your soft palm?

Could she dance on your little fingers?

She has to become strength in your arms

Does she have enough energy to climb your hip and then descend it?

She has to measure your little waist. Can she bite your milk like white tighs till they turn purple?

She has to help maintain the balance of your calf while you dance
Can she rotate with your ankle? Is it tougher than the rotations
of the earth on its axis?
Is she so sacred that she could walk with your feet because
anything which comes underneath your soul turns to paradise?
Now tell me
Is it possible for a poem ???
Just a poem ??
My Lord
How painful is your name when they take in front of me? How
lordy is your name when I take in front of 'em

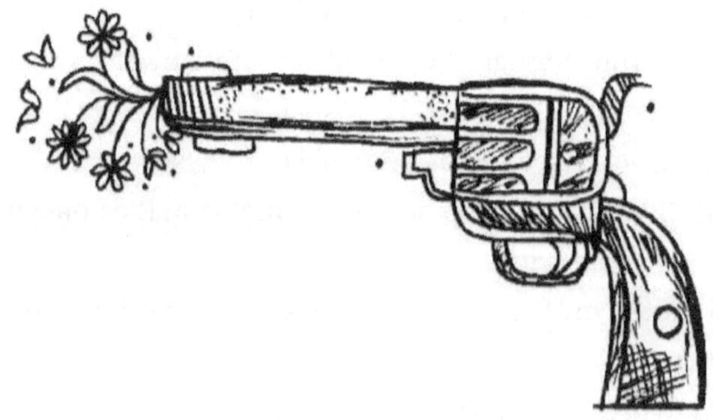

VEXATION

"You can't even bear my vexation. Imagine what's gonna happen when I tell you how much I love you."

NATURAL LOVE

It's not your fault, babe. My love for you is natural, and people take nature for granted.

POWER OF LOVE

"He just put his hand on her cheeks, and she felt like the most powerful woman on earth. She tilted her head onto his shoulder, making him the wealthiest man on earth."

LAST NIGHT

My tongue on your lips,
Your tongue on mine.
We go round and round,
Oh, goodness, that was divine. You took out the glass and poured
that red wine.
I felt that in my intestine, From sunset to sunshine. We made
love and forgot to dine.
You ate me. I ate you,
My baby, I hate you,
Why I had to wait for you,
I love you, oh great you.
You are the only boy
I will keep chasing, babe.
Last night, you were amazing, babe.

FELT CUTE

"People curse me when we meet. But I am helpless.
I hate it when they talk to you."
~lunar eclipse is a cute meet

YOU ARE HERE BUT NOT

Am I weak? Am I bold?
Can't let you go, can't even hold.
Neither feeling happy nor sad, Isn't it great? Isn't it bad? This only
thought makes me mad: how it started and where it led.
How wet this pillow, how cold this bed. But if you are still happy,
I am glad.
I hear my name in a whisper so deep,
Every fucking hour it breaks my sleep. Like the last second, you
were here, now nowhere, like God in someone's prayer.
I yearn for your touch to dissolve the ache,
In the lull of your bosom, a peace to partake.
A question, a whisper, or a glance,
I'm gonna feel worthy; just a chance.
Not for me, but for you,
My darling, this yearning brews.
In the tapestry of life where happiness ensues,
I seek your bliss, your serenity profound, a dance of souls, an
eternal round.

Halt this enchantment, cease the self-inflicted trance, Embrace the truth, in me, your destined romance. End the waltz of ambiguity, embrace clarity's decree,

I am the one, entwined, a poetic symphony.

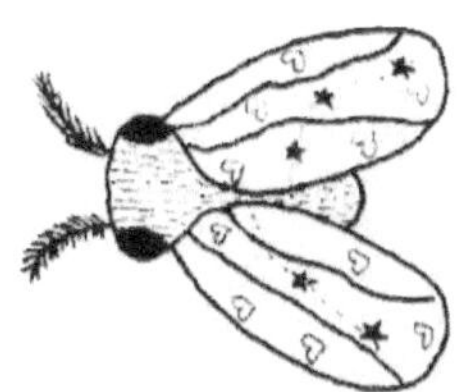

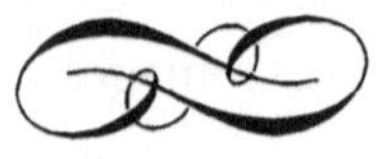

MY OINTMENT

"Apply yourself on my wounds. It heals me quicker than magic."

AU REVOIR

As you go, is it truly for forever?
What will you take with you— Your belongings or my heart?
What will you leave— Your love or your lover?
What will you take— My joy or my happiness?
What will you leave— Your memories or your scent?
What will you take— My emotions or my love?
What will you leave— Your life or my death?
What will you take—
Your lips or your cheeks?
Your kiss or your hugs?
My peace or my God?
Your touch or your warmth??
My dreams or my hopes? Irony or metaphors? Figure it out,
but please make sure to leave your scarf, hairband, or something
as valuable as life,
Please leave poetry within me so I'l can write to you.

BLAME ME

He: Baby, you killed me.
She: Nah, I killed us.

TONIGHT

"Tonight marks the final eve of your presence. Tomorrow, with the moon, you'll depart, ushering in darkness from the east, a cosmic first. Despite my efforts to impede your leave, despite my eyes pleading for a halt, you won't remain.

No mathematician on this vast earth can compute the degree of pain your decree of separation inflicts. Tomorrow, my love's star sets, perhaps never to rise again. Unwilling to accept, I ponder what comes next, what shall become of me.

Maybe I'll reach out for a few weeks; your responses may vary. The calls may reveal your learned self-sufficiency, a habit formed in the void left behind. Life, I posit, is more than a habit; it's an existence to be lived. I hope you discover a new life, distant from the chaos I sowed.

I'll cease the calls, and you won't reciprocate. I'll find the best path to survival, enduring until the end. Letters written but never sent, contemplating your fate, my fate, and the future of our love.

This last night, you're a step away, yet unreachable. How ironic that I cra this poem, unable to speak the words. Longing for your touch, tears unbridled, I implore: don't go, love. Please stay, for life, happiness, and our shared love.

No more sand trickles in the hourglass; life wanes in this body. Sensations akin to being nailed and stabbed course through; a tightening grip around my neck stifles any scream. Is this the pain of love? Must it be endured? Forget me, but I implore you to share your feelings.

What joy does this separation bring you? Is distance a necessity? If happiness resides beyond these walls, then so be it. God bless you.

Perhaps I'm undeserving yet forgive me if you can. Should you ever need me in any sense, I am here for you. Good luck. Love you. Take care."

NOT ANYMORE

I waited for you every day, hoping you would come and talk to me, but you didn't. I kept waiting, but you never showed up. Eventually, I decided to be happy without you. I started keeping myself busy, and my mind learned how to live without you. Now, I am happy this way; I don't need you anymore."

TRUE SENSE OF LOVE

If you would have chosen to walk with me, I would have taken you to heaven. I would have made you sit in the company of angels, decorated your head with stars, and placed the moon on your forehead. I would have freed you.

Seeing you free from the illusions of this world, I myself would have been freed. I would have made you God, and by worshipping you, I would have become a God. I would have emptied your mind and lit the lamp of love in your heart, with the light of which you would have become love yourself. A zone of love would be formed around you with no limits. If you could hear, it would be only love; if you could see, it would be only love. If you could smell it, it would be love. If you could feel it, it would be only love.

When the only thing that existed in the cosmos for you was love, had my love been more visible, and you would have chosen to love me, walking holding my hand, then we would have truly been in love.

BANANA REPUBLIC

"She is the state; I am a citizen. The rest, you know. My rights are being deprived."

FIRST POEM

Not in the greed of power,
Nor is the need of his bread.
He must not be a courtier trying to impress his lord,
Mustn't be a coward who fears death,
Mustn't be afraid of rebirth or judgement.
He mustn't be ambitious for the heavens or earth
He can't be a believer in faith or a devotee praising his god,
He must be sitting by a pond,
Watching the moon's shadow in the water, Listening to the music of his soul and the song of the nightingale. A leaf must have detached from the tree and must have disturbed the water.
Then, he suddenly must have seen her face. The first poem on earth must have been written for a girl like you by a boy like me in love."

NUSQUAMA

"Your love is like Eutopia, sweetheart.
So beautiful to believe but too good to be TRUE."

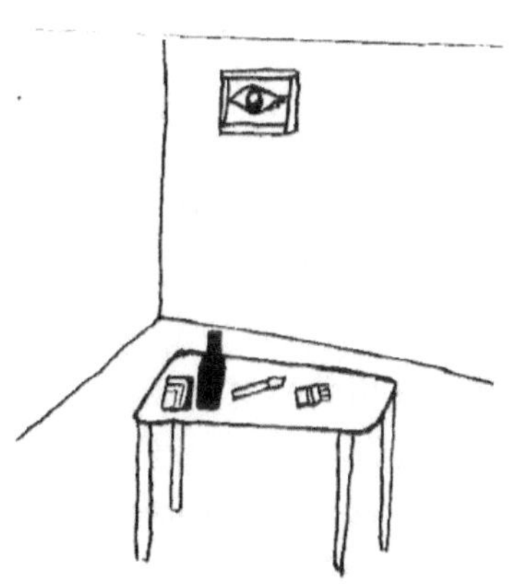

LAST PAGES

In the shadows of farewell, a poignant tale, a narrative of love, a ship set to sail.

Pages turning, heartache in each line,

As cherished moments, like chapters, decline.

The ache of parting, a bittersweet song,

A symphony of emotions, playing strong.

Your love, a story, in my heart confined,

Yet destined to leave, like the closing bind.

A favourite book, with only pages few,

Each word is a heartbeat, a farewell to pursue. Reading through the pain, words etched in tears,

The imminent separation, a cascade of fears.

As you reach the end, like turning a key, the person departs, and the book is set free. In the library of memories, she finds her shelf, a cherished novel remembered in oneself.

Talking of her, as one recalls a good book, each chapter revisited a longing look.

Her absence, a void, a literary theme,

Yet met in moments, like a dream. Once in a blue moon, like a random rhyme, her presence revisited, a fleeting time.

A page turned, a memory unfurls,
Love story is written in the hearts of two worlds.

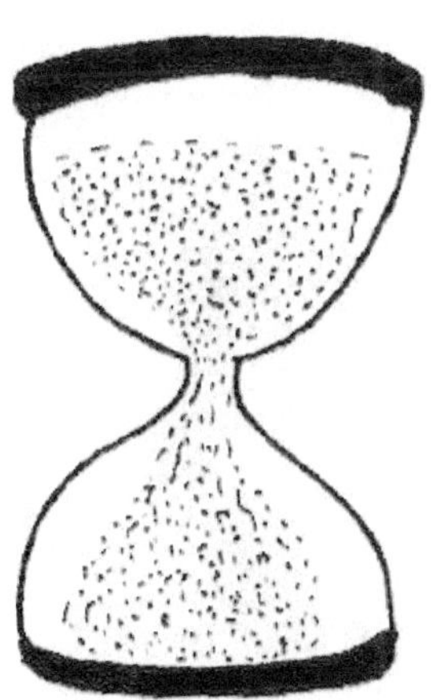

YOU ARE MYSELF

I am happy within myself, I am sad within myself, I am angry within myself, I am pleased within myself. But I share all this with you because I feel you within myself."

FIREFLIES

I released fireflies from the jar and filled your memories in my
heart,
It got lighted,
Me enlightened.

PLANT A TREE

I will sow the seeds of love. I will go to my village and plant a tree in the name of your love. Whoever sits in the shade of that tree will be transformed by love.

GIVE YOUR BEST

Your last kiss couldn't quench my thirst. Your last gaze failed to turn me into a flower. Your last hug didn't set me free. Come back once again to give your best."

NO THING

"Maybe you've earned something. Maybe you've lost something.
BUT I
I've lost nothing.
I lost everything."

CONFLICTS

I am not so headstrong and wilful. It's not easy to be stubborn. So please don't talk to me again. I am full of anger.

I'll rebuke uh, I will vituperate uh, I'll fight with uh and I'll fall in love again.

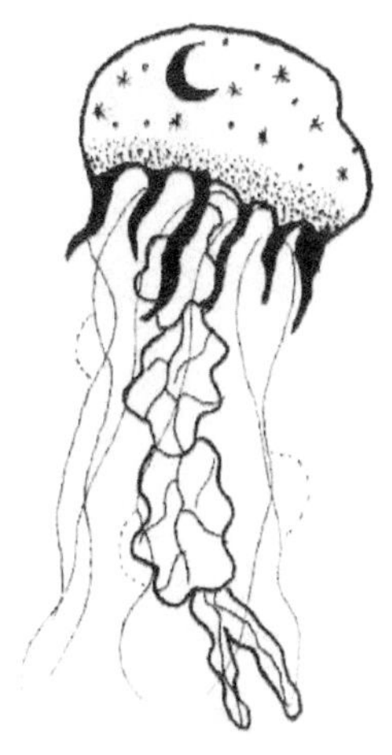

BLOSSOM UNSEEN

All the flowers of our youth have withered,
It's a pity; it happened because the flowers never bloomed.

RESPONSIBLE LOVER

I won't forget my responsibilities in love. I can't forget to love while holding responsibilities. I have a love for my responsibilities, and loving you is my responsibility."

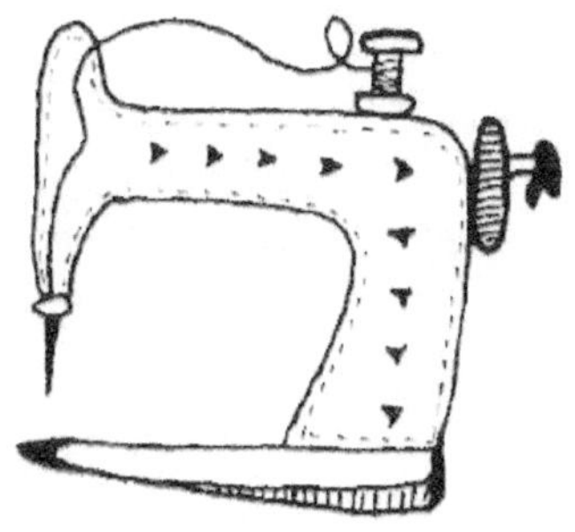

EMBERS WITHIN

So much warmth, so much anger, can exist in a body,
Don't perceive that body as just a body; call it a fragment of the
sun.

LET ME GO

Enough, don't say something now,
Sorrow had already gripped me. You gave me some moments
And the world took some away
If it's love, then dance away
If it's anger, just drink it up
If it's a complaint, then die with it
If it's pain, just live through it.

REGRET

When you used to sing for me,
I regret that I didn't record you.
When you used to kiss me, I regret why I didn't melt. When you used to recite for me, I regret why I didn't write.
When you used to be wine,
I regret why I didn't drink. When you used to hold my hand, I regret why I didn't dare. When you used to play with me, I regret why I didn't lose.
When you used to cry,
I regret why I didn't weep.
When you used to write poetry on my thighs, I regret why I didn't get it tattooed. When you used to hold me in your arms,
I regret why I didn't die.

CRUMBLE

My world withers away every day. Now even this room seems too vast. Summoning courage to open this door feels like an ordeal, and a century passes before stepping outside. Your every dream feels incredibly beautiful at the beginning, then suddenly my eyes well up. I regret pushing you away, wondering why I compelled you to leave. Perhaps, I have another heart where only you beat. There are other veins where you flow. One life I live with you and another without you.

LIGHT PEN POETRY

"After a million years you texted me my love
After a million years i turned on lights in my room"

OH !! MFERCY

Oh, this forehead! Oh, these brows!

Oh, these eyelashes! Oh, mercy! These lake-like eyes, their water,

Sometimes spills, oh, mercy!

Oh, this crooked nose! Oh, these cheeks!

Oh, these lips! Oh, mercy!

The breath, a storm, tears like rain,

Whose shelter should we seek now, oh, mercy!

Oh, this body! Oh, these colours!

Oh, this fragrance! Oh, mercy! These locks, like clouds, their shadow, Whose else's desire, oh, mercy!

The walk, like a peacock, the gaze, like a deer, oh dear !!! Oh, mercy!

Oh, this girl! Oh, this girl!

Oh my, oh, this girl! Oh, mercy!

YOUR HABITAT

Listen to this river that flows; listen to the bangles I wore. Listen
to the tinkling or listen to the jingling.
Listen to the heartbeat of this earth,
Everyone is wounded, everyone is captivated by you.
Behind the curtain of my eyes,
you reside
in every dream of mine.

REAL QUICK

Few things are so instant,
Few things are so natural,
And nothing is gradual.

SHE

There was a girl, similar to other girls, but to me, she seemed like GOD.

Sometimes, she seemed as calm as a lake. Sometimes, she seemed as disturbed as an ocean. Sometimes, she moved with grace like a peacock.

Sometimes, she stayed still like a tree. There was an enchantment in her words,

No one had the same charm in their speech.

I am ready to talk to you girls,

If you can talk like her.

SO TRUE

"You are my truth, dear,
And God knows God's truth."

YOU ARE A GEM

"She belongs to neither this earth nor this era. "

YOUR NAME

On a leaf, I wrote your name,
When I turned back, it became a poem.
To imprint, to erase, to hide, to read,
For me, this matter became a dilemma.
The path we used to meet on,
I heard on that path it became a mosque
People ask about the destiny of my love; like Ranjha, I've become
a wanderer.
Why did I bring love to my heart,
For a lifetime, I've become a patient. The sand that came from
your footsteps, what magic did it carry?
It became the sky.
On the desert, I wrote your name,
Selling and selling, it became an ocean.
What I wrote on my heart, your name,

It didn't stay heart anymore, and it became a temple.

PETALS

I consider calling those lips just lips a disrespect.
Don't call those lips lips; call them the envy of roses.

WILTED HORIZONS

Silent sit the branches,
No bird is soaring,
Have their wings been severed,
Or have they all feasted their fill?
No wind is blowing, no cloud is rising,
What kind of mourning is this? Has someone died?
The crops that filled this field
were thriving until yesterday,
Why is it barren now? Who has deserted it?
No river flows, no fire ignites the jungle,
Eyes have dried up, and blood has turned cold.
Has desire been extinguished, or has love died?
In what fear are you, and from whom am I scared?
No fragrance lingers in the air,
Nor do any colours remain,
Does it mean you have died, or have I perished?

YOUUUU

You are my golden dream,
The garden of my happiness,
The light of my sorrows,
The lamp of my hopes.
Do you wonder who you are to me?
People ask what am I to you
I know I am nothing to you,
But without you, I am nothing at all.
You are my love, my passion, my God, my worship. To embellish me, in your hands, to wither, in your hands. You are my decoration, my creation, my love, my world.
You are my obsession, my life,
You are my universe.
Every moment spent with you,
Every moment remembered with you,
Every moment seen with you,
Every moment awaited with you,
Every moment awaited for you,
Every moment saved for you All those moments are in my memory, and they never tire. I never tire of looking at it, and I will never tire.

You are my pain, my incomplete journey; you are my wounds,
my heartache.
You are my answer, my question.
You are my being, my existence.
You are my life, my identity.
You, my love, my everything,
You are my beloved, my destiny
My fate lies in the lines of your palms
All my happiness is connected to you
Leaving nights behind, you rise in my eyes
Like the redness surpassing the sun, you speak
You pull the moon towards yourself
You've drawn the stars towards you
Swear on God, you are a distraction
When I saw you, even silence didn't listen
Without your memories, every moment feels empty
You are my well-being, my current state
From you, my melodies and rhythms emerge
You are my music, my song, my soulmate
You are my youth, my world
You are my God, my Lord
Every night, there's intoxication
Every morning, there's joy;
Do you know, my dear, what you mean to me?
Just as there's a morning, there's a night;
Similarly, for me, your face is like the morning
You are the one for me
For whom the moon shines, for whom darkness turns into light

For whom nights exist
For whom the body craves
When you walk, the fragrance spreads
My heart recognises you when someone talks about happiness
You are the solitary thought of my loneliness

you

SACRED FUSION

Loving you is sole purpose of my soul.

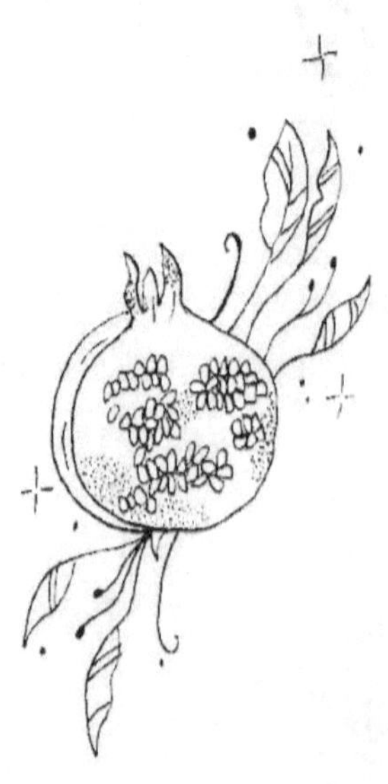

FAITH

There's no news of rights,
But one truth is certain,
A love that is true,
That I keep in my heart,
And won't reveal,
It's as solid as a hundred times ground.
Even then, if she comes to know,
Let the stream of love burst,
Let her kiss my forehead; let her touch my words. Then only I
could have faith in that God,
Whom no one has ever seen,
Who resides within the stones,
I haven't bowed my head.

ME/HE

"He has become me,
I have become him,
So, who are you talking to? Please be specific,
Oh, my bad; how could you be !!??

LOVE LANGUAGE

In the language of love,
There are no final words,
Emotions are precious,
And sorrows are endured.

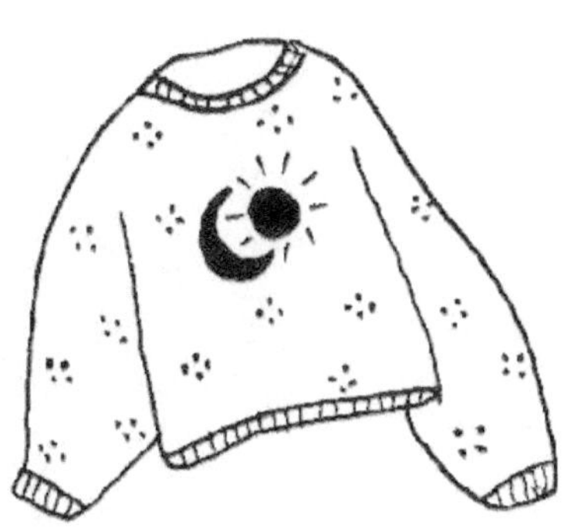

WORTH WRITING

Rest are beautiful, but you are poetic.

SYMPHONY OF SKIN

Spring has brought flowers again, my beloved; the search is intense. Through twists and turns, I seek you, In the tangle of my locks, my love.

Handle the locks with care,

Sweetheart, and place this veil behind my ear.

Kiss my senses away,

Kiss my pain away,

I want to sink in your skin. Your fingers were something; they were something else.

I want to eat those digits.

I want to flow in your veins, just as you do in mine.

You alone are my destiny; you alone are my journey.

You seem like the ultimate truth to me,

It seems like you are the greater purpose for which I was born on this earth.

I DARE

"In every fucking life, whenever I see you, I am gonna fall for you."

WORRY

Worry about this girl if you dare,
Then, face the consequences, my love. Worry about this girl if
you dare, then this girl won't worry anymore.

DENIAL

Asking me to stop caring for you is like asking the earth to become infertile.

Asking me not to die for you is like asking the sun not to burn.

Asking me to stop worrying for you is like asking trees not to provide shadow.

Asking me to stop loving you is like asking the heart to stop beating.

Asking me to stop protecting you is like asking the Himalayas not to protect Mother India.

A steadfast bond, forever pure.

Through the seasons, our love shall endure, Asking me to stop, a whimsical goal, you are the sole purpose of my soul.

Asking me to give up on you is like asking a river to give up on its water.

FELT LOVED

You called me unique when they were making fun of my hair.
You have cleaned my body, my vomit, my tears.
You always call me BABY when I'm a mess!
You are truly a prince who made a country girl the princess,
I am not aware of the actual definition of beautiful
But the way you make me feel is beyond beautiful
- feeling of getting loved

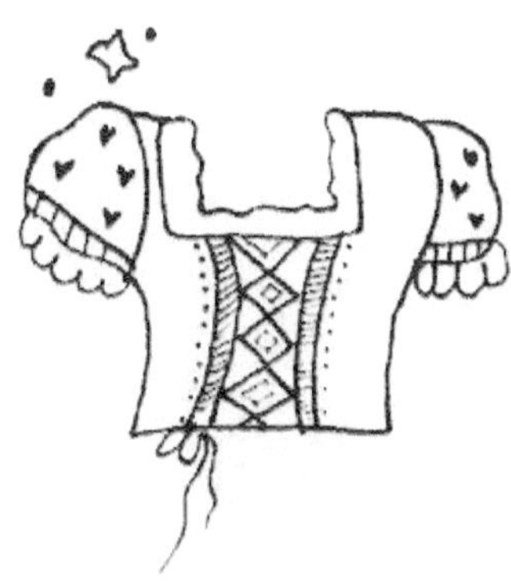

CANDLE MADE OF SAND

You light me up, and I melt
Not because I am burning
But to make you smell the aroma of what a first meet feels like
You are the first rain on my sand
- my heart is a candle made up of sand

OLD SKOOL

The way I put my lipstick stamps on paper,
For you, knitting a matching sweater
Blushing out about how stupidly I am into you
Cooking your favourite meals in a queue
Lighting up scented ones
Not one! A million tons. Why all this..?
Cause baby, I am an old-school lover.
It makes me dance when you adore my love for you with your
eyes and shiny face
- old-school lover

BLESSED

Thy look at us
with eyes full of desire
to have a love that
him and I share.

WROIT

If it's wrong or right
Will be dark
But right now, so bright
Insecurities gone
Dusk feels dawn
Without the sun, is there any moon?
Maybe it won't end
Or end up so soon
Even when I am free,
Always rooted up like a tree
Not as calm as you,
Tied up, still so free!

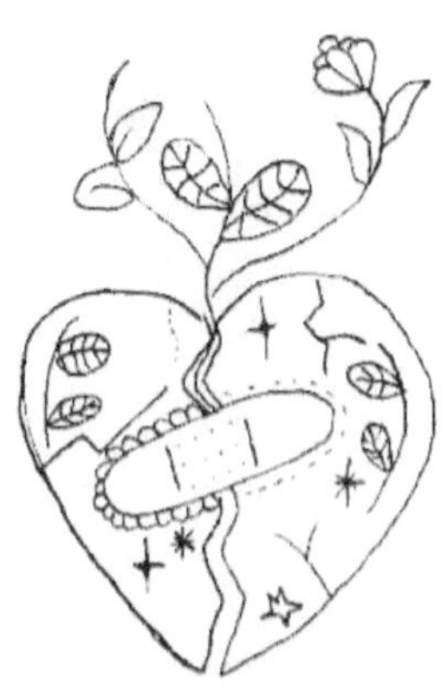

WASTED LOVE

"He was drunk enough to propose me with an imaginary flower in his hand. "

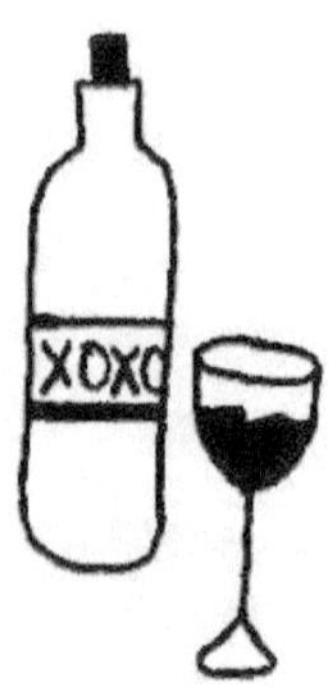

MAGIC SPEAKS

To the most magical night ever:
He armed my waist
I turned my face,
And magic happened;
The idea of getting touched
Was dark before
But it suddenly got lightened,
Our breaths got warmest
Lips became charmest
And fear got frightened,
We were still into it
and that very moment, it
was literally a twist
- magic speaks.

ANAGAPESIS

I gave you love,
I gave you pain,
When you were crying- I gave you my vein
I crushed you to make you brave. Oh, my prey!
It's how I predate. I'll stop hunting from now on...
Even if I'm dying, that love is gone !!

AMBUSCADE

"Babe, that was an ambuscade."

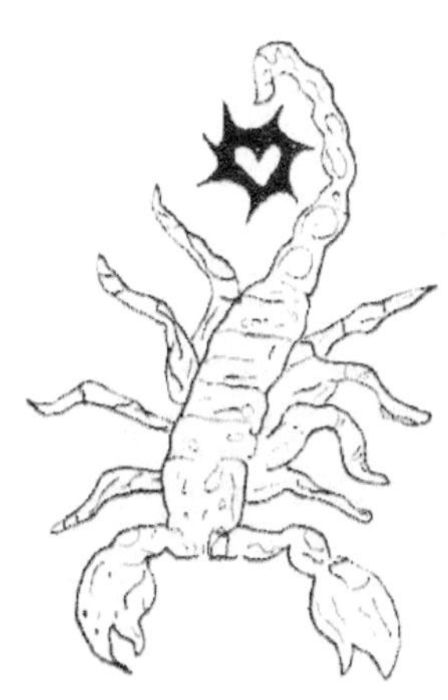

BURNING HOME

"While burning my every ounce, thy called me home."

ODE TO NATURE

"Hey, prettiest tyrant, why did you create us?!
To destroy you or to destroy us? "

TO EMPRESS

"I thought I was just a flower
That got lost. Oh, dear me!
I am bougainvillea
I have reach, I have atoms, I have parts
Even unnoticed ones where life camouflage."

LOOK AT THE MIRROR, HONEY

"Shiny eyes, bright tears, insane smile. You are behind the mirror hearing a soft voice... Voice of thoughts and thoughts never lie. They shall not just pass... they should be taken care of and nourished."

LET'S WONDER

"We are so lost with the things that we are done and over with.
Are you really over and done?
Haha.
We never get rid of old things.
You, too, wonder, right..?!
Because remembering stays,
Like wild weed breaking waves, either good or evil, it just stays."

TRANQUILLISE

"Sit around the cascade,

Flick your digits with petals of your favourite flower and stroll around.

Take some time from your hooligan psych ward, expel all the irritants, and smile in numbness.

Make your zygomatic flesh.

Blushy out of cantaloupe.

Do stare at the tree with red leaves,

And collect all the aesthetics until your tiredness gets you high,

And feel this stoned life

With infinite loops in a single string

ESSENCE

Tears fade
Words omit history
But there is no escape door, my love
Heartache! It comes with a smile, too.
And people predict foolishly..!!

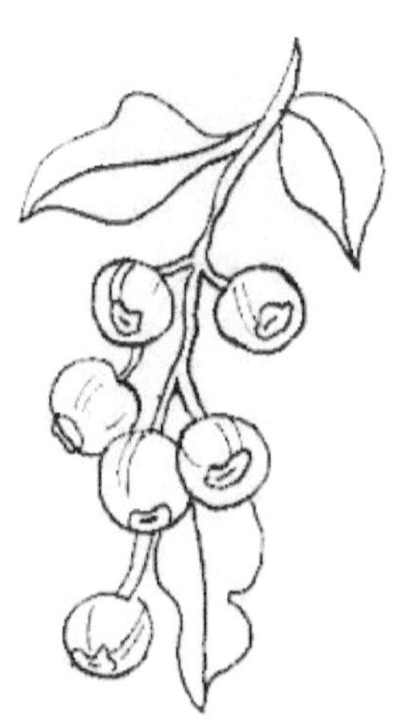

HOO ALLAH

"Everything I had is now lost to you. You made me forget even my prophets."

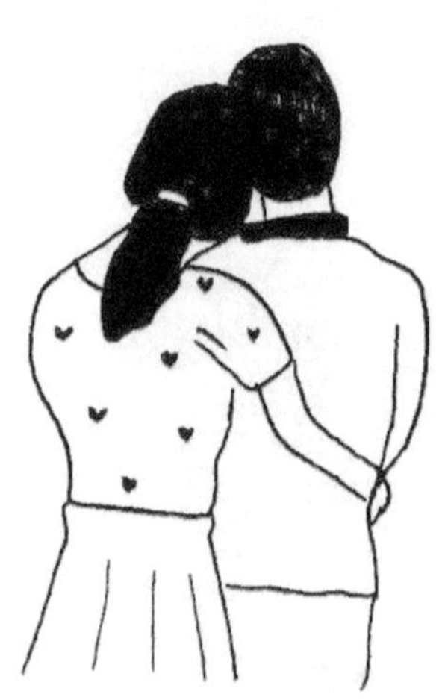

EVERYTHING IS BEAUTIFUL

"Rays over my rays,
What else does hope feel like?
What else do I need to be to look more alive?!
I will look for it,
Even the dead and dry flower
Reminds me of the prettiest bookmark!"

WE ARE ALIKE

"We cipher human - can grasp together.
From not knowing - we vibe together.
When I was a runner - you were my catcher.
Our life is a blunder - maybe a disaster.
Can grab an umbrella - and go together.
Hey you! Usually gossamer,
Ice, fire, and vapour & a pearl in oyster.
I will love your aura forever."

SO BEAUTIFUL

He: You are so beautiful
Me: Make me believe that
Then he kissed me.

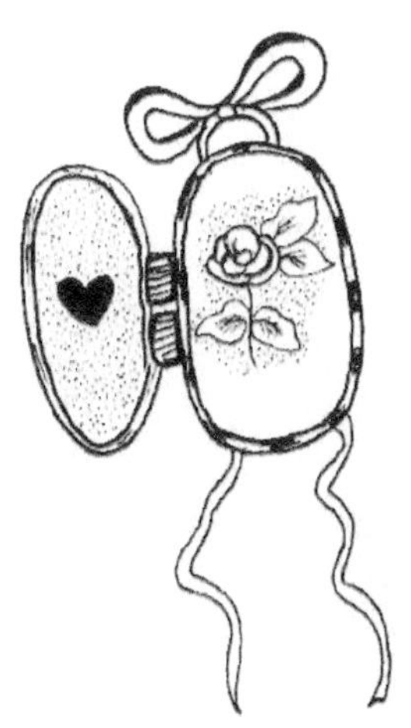

LONG LIVE REVOLUTION

"………you know; that's what love stands for. That's what we stand for," he interrupted.

He: "But what do we stand against?"

She: "Uhmmm."

He: "Yeah, what do we stand against?"

She: "Against what??"

He: "Everything. If we are in love, we have to stand against 'everything.' So, do I have your back?"

She grabbed his hand.

He: "Dear Comrade, say something."

She: "Long Live Revolution."

LOVELISM

"Does somebody know Marx? I'm not getting labour for my love."

LET'S ACT

"Imitating happiness
For a while,
But your thought
Fondled me,
set me high and dry
And I am a shrivelled petal again."

THOUGHTFULLY ROOTED

"Thoughts, thoughts everywhere, nor anything to think.
Full of them, share to whom?
I will get nothing but empathy.
What if this breaks me?
Is it possible for a bud to leave its roots?
The roots that love her in their way,
That is what she hates the most."

PRISON OF GOLD

"I would rather like to be a traveller with no penny than to be a rich girl under town arrest."

TÚ

Hey, it's you,
Sitting beside the window And watching out.
There was so much to look for, but it's you I was thinking about.
Death is not the goal, but you are the graveyard I want to die in.
You are so fevered with nature, and I am barely a moon person.
Now that I have met you, I am in love with every part of it: the
habits, the old, the new, because hey! It's just you."

PECADORA

"Becoming a butterfly
It's not just a distance to cover from birth leaf to the sky
It's all about thorns, the foes to fight with, and then the cruel job
of sucking the sweetness out of flowers
And flying out of all regrets."

LÉITHEOIR

\# why poem???
~ poems are shameless,
Yet we read them to unhide the pain we hide on our faces
Poems don't influence us; they really cannot!
But we fall for wording
Our emotions get words from that
What else could a human ask?

HAKUNA MATATA

"Do things without regret,
Cause you know you won't regret it.
Like the moon, I am tossed in your open sky with songs and laughter.
You are a cocoon with a blushy valve,
Hidden amongst the leaves of my body.
Walking out to the self-world,
Who will cherish whoever I am,
Against all oddities."

BILINGUAL

"Get disloyal to the world
Who is bilingual on your face."

AGAIN????

Oh me! Oh no !!
Hey, you!!! Hey no !!!!

LE SAUVEUR

I have listened to all poems, I have listened to all verselets
I have heard the sonnets of forests
I have heard all stories, I have listened to all couplets, I have
listened to all tales.
Whatever has been said, whatever has not been said,
I have heard the silence of lips and the voices of hearts. But I
swear, sweetheart, nothing was as complete as your words,
I have seen the world; I have not seen the world, but I have seen
nothing like those two eyes.
It is your gravity which does not let the moon suck all the love
from this planet." It's you for whom this wind is blowing.
Whoever is building roads wants to reach you.
Whoever has eyes wants to see you.
It is you from whom this spring is blooming.
Won't these leaves be untouched by you until autumn?
In your search, cranes take flights.
For you, these mountains are erupting. For you, everything
exists.

I, too, could have fallen for this hell, luckily saved by you, who tied us by THE KNOT OF PINKIE FINGERS."